First World War
and Army of Occupation
War Diary
France, Belgium and Germany

39 DIVISION
118 Infantry Brigade
Black Watch (Royal Highlanders)
5th Battalion
1 January 1916 - 15 March 1916

WO95/2591/2

The Naval & Military Press Ltd
www.nmarchive.com
Published in association with The National Archives

Published by

The Naval & Military Press Ltd

Unit 10 Ridgewood Industrial Park,

Uckfield, East Sussex,

TN22 5QE England

Tel: +44 (0) 1825 749494

www.naval-military-press.com

www.nmarchive.com

This diary has been reprinted in facsimile from the original. Any imperfections are inevitably reproduced and the quality may fall short of modern type and cartographic standards.

© **Crown Copyright**
Images reproduced by permission of The National Archives, London, England, 2015.

Contents

Document type	Place/Title	Date From	Date To
Heading	WO95/2591/2 5bn Black Watch (Royal High Landers) Jan-Mar 1916 39 Div-118 Inf Bde		
Heading	51st Division 154th Infy Bde 39 Division 118 Bde 1-5th Bn Black Watch (Roy. Highlanders) Jan-Feb 1916		
Heading	1/5th R. Highn Pioneers From 8th Division To 159th Bde 51st Div Jan 51 Div 6.1.16 Vol XIII		
War Diary	In The Field	01/01/1916	29/02/1916
Heading	39 Division 118 Bde 5 Bn Black Watch (R Highlanders) 1916 Jan-1916 Mar From 8 Division 24 Bde Amalgamated		
Heading	39th Division 118th Infantry Brigade 4/5th Black Watch 1/5th Battalion The Black Watch March 1916		
Heading	1/5 Royal Hrs Vol XV		
Miscellaneous	A.G.S Officer at the Base, Central Registry Rouen.	04/04/1916	04/04/1916
War Diary	In The Field	01/03/1916	15/03/1916

WO95/2591 — 2

5 Bn Black Watch (Royal Highlanders)

Jan – Mar 1916

39 Div — 118 Inf Bde

ATTACHED } 51ST DIVISION
154TH INFY BDE

39 DIVISION
118 BDE

1-5TH BN BLACK WATCH
(ROY.HIGHLANDERS)
JAN-FEB 1916

FROM 8 DIV 24 BDE

1/5th R. Highrs.

from 8th Division Pioneers to 154th Bde 51st Div. Jan
51st Div ~~July~~
6.1.16

Vol XIII

154/51

January 1916

1/5th Bn. The Black Watch

WAR DIARY or INTELLIGENCE SUMMARY

Army Form C. 2118.

Place	Date	Hour	Summary of Events and Information	Remarks and references to Appendices
In the Field	1st		New Years Day. Being a day of celebration, the Battalion did not parade. Messages of greetings were sent to & received from different Units in the Division. Weather very squally.	
	2nd		Numbers 1 & 2 Coys. paraded for Divine Service at 11-30 a.m. at Reading Room. Orders having been received that the Battalion was being relieved at LA MOTTE by another Battalion; Nos 3 & 4 Coys. marched from LA RUE DE BOIS billets at 1 p.m. and went into billets beside Nos 1 & 2 Coys. at STEENBECQUE at 4 p.m. 2 platoons of No 3 Coy. took over billets in RUE NEUVE. Weather very bad. 1 Officer rejoined off leave.	
	3rd		Nos 1 & 2 Coys. paraded at 10 a.m. & 2 p.m. for Infantry training under Coy. Arrangements. Nos 3 & 4 Coys. paraded at 11 a.m. in football field for inspection by C.O. and at 2 p.m. under Coy. Arrangements. 15 O.Rs. proceeding on leave this evening to United Kingdom.	
	4th		At 9.15 a.m. in grass field adjoining No 1 Coys billet on the STEENBECQUE - MERVILLE road the Battalion was inspected by Major-General H. HUDSON, C.B., C.I.E. G.O.C. 8th Division. 21 Officers & 417 other ranks were on parade. The Battalion was drawn up in 3 sides of a square and received the General with the General Salute. The General said he had come to bid them good-bye, as the Battalion left his Division on the 6th inst., and to say how well the Battalion had done in the 14 months they had been in FRANCE with the 8th Division; how courageously they had fought; and how well & cheerfully they had worked as a Pioneer Battalion since November. He wished them all good luck. At 9-30 a.m. the Corps Commander, General Pulteney inspected the Battn. He inspected the ranks & bade the Battalion good-bye, thanking them for their good services and saying he would look for reports of further good work by the Battalion, which he was sure it would perform. The General shook hands with the Officers. The Battalion marched past the General in Column of Route.	

1/5th Bn. The Black Watch
January 1916

WAR DIARY or INTELLIGENCE SUMMARY

Army Form C. 2118.

(Erase heading not required.)

Place	Date	Hour	Summary of Events and Information	Remarks and references to Appendices
In the Field	5th		The Battalion paraded under Company arrangements.	
	6th		The Battalion left Bn. Hd. Qrs. STEENBECQUE at 7.30 a.m. in dull weather. On crossing the Railway the Battalion marched past the 8th Division R.E's drawn up to give the Battalion a farewell cheer. On the journey to THIENNES the C.R.E 8th Division met the Battalion & bade good-bye to it. The Battalion entrained at THIENNES (breakfast being taken at the station). No. 1 Coy provided the loading party. The Battalion arrived at IONSEAU (near AMIENS) about 8 p.m. & detrained. No. 2 Coy. provided the unloading party. Dinner was taken at IONSEAU. Battalion then marched to COISY, some 8 miles march & billeted there.	
	7th		Battalion employed improving billets & cleaning up after journey.	
	8th		Battalion paraded under Coy arrangements at 7.30 a.m. 10 a.m. & 2 p.m. 1 O. & 21 O.Rs. left on short leave.	
	9th		Battalion paraded for Divine Service in School grounds, COISY at 10-30 a.m. Reading Room opened in School Room. 4 Officers rejoined off leave. 1 Officer proceeded on Short Leave.	
	10th		Battalion paraded at 7.30 a.m. 10 a.m. & 2 p.m. under Coy arrangements. The weather continues fine.	
	11th		Battalion paraded at 12 noon & was inspected by Brigadier-General. C. Stewart, C.M.G, commanding 154th Infantry Brigade. The Brigadier inspected the Battalion & then addressed them, saying how glad he was to welcome such an experienced Battalion to his Brigade. He termed it, "A most creditable parade". Parade Strength 15 Officers 429 O.Rs. 1 Prisoner rejoined C/E G. Ballinger, from Base under escort.	
	12th		Lieut. J.J. McL. Mills joined the Battalion to-day. He reverts to rank of 2nd Lieut. Parades as before.	
	13th		Regimental Canteen opened today. Parades as before.	
	14th		Parades as usual. Lieut. DUKE & 2nd Lieut. MILLS, 2 sgts. & 16 men left Battalion to join Brigade M.G. Coy. attached to 154th Infantry Brigade.	

January 1/5th Bn. The Black Watch 1916

WAR DIARY or INTELLIGENCE SUMMARY

Army Form C. 2118.

(Erase heading not required.)

Place	Date	Hour	Summary of Events and Information	Remarks and references to Appendices
In the Field	15th		Parades in morning at 10 a.m. Half holiday granted to Battalion on Saturdays in future. 1 Officer + 21 O.Rs. granted leave of absence.	
	16th		Battalion paraded for Divine Services at 10-30 a.m. + 7 p.m (voluntary).	
	17th		Parades as usual.	
	18th		Battalion paraded as usual. The following list of honours was announced. No 2025 Pte. J. DAVIDSON No 2 Coy. + No 547 Pte. GRAHAM, No 4 Coy. D.C.M. 2nd Lieut. G.A. GRANT. Military Cross.	
	19th		Parades as before. Capt W.I. MITCHELL seconded + attached to 8th Division Signals. 1 Officer rejoined off Leave.	
	20th		Parades as before. No 3 + 4 Coys. were at Divisional Baths.	
	21st		Battalion took part in Tactical Scheme + defended the village of COISY against attacks by 4th BLACK WATCH + 4th CAMERONS. The weather was dull but dry. The Brigade (less 1 Battalion) took part in scheme.	
	22nd		Parades as usual. 2nd Lieut Paterson + 28 O.Rs. granted leave of Absence.	
	23rd		Battalion paraded for Divine Service at 10-30 a.m.	
	24th		Parades: - No 2, 3, + 4 Coys. Route March + No 1 Coy. at the ranges. No 1899 Pte. DICKSON attended Divisional Cooking Class. 1 Officer Lieut J. McP. Duker granted special leave till 8-2-16.	
	25th		Battalion paraded at 12-15 p.m. for inspection by G.O.C. 51st (High). Division. The G.O.C. inspected the Battalion. Parade state = 17 Officers, 357 O.Rs. The Battalion marched past in Column of Route. 1 Officer rejoined off leave.	
	26th		Parades as usual.	
	27th		Col. MILLAR V.D. took command of 4th CAMERONS + 4th SEAFORTH Highlanders, and defended for a time N.E. of COISY against attack by 4th The BLACK WATCH. Battalion did not take part but provided 5 Officers as Umpires: - Capt. G.S. RAE, Capt. A.H.M. WEDDERBURN, Capt. N.K. TAYLOR, Lieut. R.F.D. BRUCE, + Lieut. J.R. MURRAY.	

1/5th Bn. The Black Watch

WAR DIARY
INTELLIGENCE SUMMARY
(Erase heading not required.)

January 1916

Army Form C. 2118.

Instructions regarding War Diaries and Intelligence Summaries are contained in F. S. Regs., Part II. and the Staff Manual respectively. Title pages will be prepared in manuscript.

Place	Date	Hour	Summary of Events and Information	Remarks and references to Appendices
In the Field	28th		Battalion parades as usual. Lieut. J.R. Murray proceeded on leave today.	
	29th		No 1 + 2 Coys. took part in tactical scheme at Divl. Grenade School, under Lieut. Bruce. No 3 + 4 Coys. route march under Capt. Taylor. Half Holiday. Lieuts. Vaughan, T 2nd Lieut. Ritchie joined the Battalion. 2nd Lieut. McBeth & 28 O.Rs. granted leave.	
	30th		Lieut. R.L.K. Miss I joined the Battalion + reverts to 2nd Lieut. The Battalion paraded for Divine Service, at 11 a.m. the Brigadier being present.	
	31st		Parades as usual. 1. O.R. joined after evacuation.	

During the month the Battalion football team won the 154th Infantry Brigade competition, winning 2 and drawing 1 game. They were defeated in 1st round of the Divisional Competition by the 7th Black Watch after a very keen game. Score: 2-0.

Summary of Casualties during month.

	Killed		Wounded		Missing		Sick		Total	
	O	O.Rs.	O	O.Rs.	O	O.Rs.	O	O.Rs.	O	O.Rs.
Admitted to Hospital	-	-	-	-	-	-	-	40	-	40
Rejoined from Hospital	-	-	-	-	-	-	-	14	-	14

Strength of Battalion

Strength of Battn. at beginning of month = 31 Officers + 648 O.Rs.
" " " end of month = 31 Officers + 625 O.Rs.

R. H. Millar Lieut. Col.
C.O. 1/5th Bn. The Black Watch
In the Field
4-2-16

1/5th Battn. The Black Watch.

WAR DIARY or INTELLIGENCE SUMMARY

February 1916

Joined 118 Bde 27/2/16

Army Form C. 2118.

Place	Date	Hour	Summary of Events and Information	Remarks and references to Appendices
In the Field	1st		At 11-45 a.m. the Battalion attended a gas demonstration by 3rd Army Expert. After a lecture on the tube helmet & gas generally used by the enemy, the Battalion passed through a room filled with gas. No ill effects were felt by any of the men. Other parades were as usual.	
	2nd		Battalion paraded at full strength, and as part of the 154th Inf. Brigade went for a route march, the distance being twelve miles. The order of march was 4th Black Watch, 5th Black Watch, 4th Seaforths & 4th Camerons. One man of the 5th fell out owing to his fainting. The dress was full marching order, (service dress)	
	3rd		The Battalion took part in Brigade Manoeuvres. The Battalion paraded on the COISY-RAINNEVILLE road, and proceeded to attack trenches at CARDONETTE. The 4th & 5th Black Watch attacked against the 4th Seaforth Highlanders. The weather was fine & dry.	
	4th		The Battalion paraded at 7.15, 10 a.m. & 2 p.m. under Coy. arrangements. Lieut. VAUGHAN & 10 O.Rs. proceeded to Lewis Gun School, WISQUES for instruction.	
	5th		The Battalion paraded in COISY and marched to some open ground on the COISY-CARDONETTE Road, and went through Artillery formation movements. Capt. RAE was in command. 2/Lieut YARROW & 22 O.Rs. were granted leave of absence from 5th to 13th inst.	

Aw. Blair-Imrie

1/5th Battn. The Black Watch
February WAR DIARY 1916
INTELLIGENCE SUMMARY.
(Erase heading not required.)

Army Form C. 2118.

Place	Date	Hour	Summary of Events and Information	Remarks and references to Appendices
In the Field	6th		The Battalion paraded for Divine Service in School Grounds Coisy at 10-30 a.m. The Brigadier being present. 31 O.R. joined the Battalion as reinforcements.	
	7th		The Battalion as part of the 154th Inf Brigade, vacated the billets in Coisy and marched to new billets in La Neuville, Corbie, (Sheet 17, Amiens). The order of march was 5th Black Watch, 4th Seaforths, 4th Camerons, & 4th Black Watch. No men fell out in a march of twelve miles.	
	8th		Battalion paraded as usual at 7-15, 10 a.m, & 2 p.m. under coy. arrangements. The afternoon parade was spent in improvement of billets. 2nd Lieut. TAIRD joined the Battalion to-day.	
	9th		As usual. Nomenclature of Coys. altered to read, No 1 Coy. "A", No 2 Coy. "B", No 3 Coy. "C", No 4 Coy. "D".	
	10th		Battalion paraded as usual.	
	11th		Recreation Room opened at La Neuville. 2nd Lieut. GUTHRIE granted leave from 12th to 20th inst. Three lads (under 17) transferred to Home Establishment.	
	12th		Battalion paraded strong and took part in Brigade Tactical Scheme. The 5th defended some high ground north of CORBIE against the attack of the 4th Seaforths & 4th Black Watch. The day started wet but cleared up during the operations. 2nd Lieut HANDYSIDE & 17 O.Rs. granted leave of absence from 13th to 21st inst.	

Hew Blair Imrie
Lt Col

1/5th Batt. The Black Watch.
February 1916

WAR DIARY
or
INTELLIGENCE SUMMARY.

(Erase heading not required.)

Army Form C. 2118.

Place	Date	Hour	Summary of Events and Information	Remarks and references to Appendices
In the Field	13th		Battalion paraded as part of 154th Inf Brigade and took part in Brigade Church Service. Dress:- Drill order. Service was held in LA NEUVILLE.	
	14th		Battalion paraded as usual. Lewis Gun Team started training.	
	15th		Battalion provided working party of 400 men to build railway at DAOURS. (Amiens sheet 17). Capt. AUBERTIN (in command). Lieut. VAUGHAN, 2nd Lieut. MILL, 2nd Lieut. IAIRD were the officers detailed. The weather proved miserably wet.	
	16th		Battalion provided 300 men for work as yesterday. Lieut MURRAY assumed command of "D" Coy, vice Capt. TAYLOR on course of instruction.	
	17th		As before. 300 men employed. Lewis gunners were exempt & carried on separate training. Draft of 58 men joined Battalion from 3/5th Black Watch.	
	18th		As before. Lewis gunners & bombers exempt. Draft posted as follows:- "A" Coy. 10, "B" Coy. 17, "C" Coy. 15, "D" Coy. 16.	
	19th		Battalion allotted baths & Coys. paraded for this. Col. P.H.N. WEDDERBURN and 15 O.Rs. granted leave of absence from 20th to 28th inst. Lewis Gunners fired at the ranges in the afternoon. Bombers also paraded under Lieut. GARDYNE.	
	20th		Battalion took part in Brigade Divine Service at LA NEUVILLE at 10-30 a.m. The C.O. inspected the draft.	Alex Blair Imrie Lt Col

1/5th Batt The Black Watch
February 1916

WAR DIARY
or
INTELLIGENCE SUMMARY.
(Erase heading not required.)

Army Form C. 2118.

Instructions regarding War Diaries and Intelligence Summaries are contained in F. S. Regs., Part II. and the Staff Manual respectively. Title pages will be prepared in manuscript.

Place	Date	Hour	Summary of Events and Information	Remarks and references to Appendices
In the Field	21st		Companies paraded as usual at 7-15 a.m. & 10 a.m. The Brigadier granted Battalion half holiday to attend final of Brigade Football Cup. 5th Black Watch v Machine Gun Coy. The result being 2-1 in our favour.	
	22nd		The Battalion paraded as usual at 7-15 a.m. 10 a.m. & 2 p.m. under Company arrangements.	
	23rd		Company Parades as usual. Lieut. Col. Hew Blair Imrie, C.M.G. rejoined the Battalion. Capt & Adjt J. Kennedy also rejoined.	
	24th		Coys paraded for baths. Lieut. Col. BLAIR-IMRIE assumed command of the Battalion vice Lieut. Col. R. H. MILLAR, V.D. transferred to Home Establishment. Capt & Adjt J. Kennedy assumed the duties of Adjutant vice 2nd Lieut. LEONARD A. ELGOOD. Capt T. CRUICKSHANK rejoined the Battalion to-day.	
	25th		The Battalion paraded at 7-30 a.m. & marched to LONGEAU (some 10 or 11 miles) The roads were very hard & snow was falling, the transport experiencing a trying time. During the march snow fell heavily. "C" Coy provided escort for the transport. On arrival at the station "A" Coy & 2 platoons from "D" Coy entrained the transport and the train left at 1-30 p.m. The Battalion detrained at ST. OMER. Snow still fell heavily. "D" Coy provided the unloading party. The Battalion left ST OMER Station at 12-15 a.m and marched to RENESCURE a distance of eight miles	Appendix 1 Page 7.

Hew Blair Imrie

1/5th Battn. The Black Watch
February 1916

WAR DIARY or INTELLIGENCE SUMMARY

Army Form C. 2118.

(Erase heading not required.)

Place	Date	Hour	Summary of Events and Information	Remarks and references to Appendices
In the Field	26th		Again the Transport had great difficulty in getting along the roads and part was left at ARQUES. The Battalion proceeded to billets in RENESCURE.	
	27th		The Battalion was employed in a thorough clean up of all equipment and inspections were carried out by O.C. Coys. The C.O. went round billets at 12 noon.	
	28th		Snow still being on the ground it was impossible to have training parades and the Battalion was employed in Squad Drill & hair cutting etc.	
	29th		Companies were at the disposal of O.C. Coys. during the day. Capt T. LYALL & 64 O.Rs. joined the Battalion and were posted as follows:- "A" Coy 5. "B" Coy 5. "C" Coy 17. "D" Coy 37. Capt. J. CRUICKSHANK assumed the duties of second in command vice Capt G.S. RAE, d/d 24th inst. Capt G.S. RAE assumed the duties of O.C. "D" Coy vice Lieut J.R. MURRAY, d/d 1st March 1916. The Battalion joined the 118th Inf. Brigade, 39th Division, to day.	

Arth Blair Imrie
Lt Col

1/5th Battn. The Black Watch
February 1916.

WAR DIARY
or
INTELLIGENCE SUMMARY.
(Erase heading not required.)

Army Form C. 2118.

Place	Date	Hour	Summary of Events and Information	Remarks and references to Appendices
In the Field	29th		Summary of Casualties during month.	

	Killed		Wounded		Missing		Sick		Total	
	O	O.Rs	O	O.Rs	O	O.Rs	O	O.Rs	O	O.Rs
Admitted to Hospital	-	-	-	-	-	-	-	40	-	40
Rejoined from Hospital	-	-	-	-	-	-	-	40	-	40

Strength of Battalion

	O	O.Rs
Strength of Battn. at 1-2-16 =	31	625
Do. at 29-2-16 =	34	753
Increase	3	128

In the Field,
1-3-16.

AKnox Blair-Imrie Lieut-Col,
C.C. 1/5th Battn. The Black Watch

39 DIVISION
118 BDE

5 BN BLACK WATCH (R. HIGHLANDERS)

1916 JAN — 1916 MAR

From 8 DIV 24 BDE

TRANSFERRED WITH 4 DIV
IND KNOWN AS 4/5 BK
WITH 39 DIV 118 BDE

39th Division.
118th Infantry Brigade

4/5th BLACK WATCH

1/5th BATTALION

THE BLACK WATCH

MARCH 1916

1/5 Royal Ars
Vol XV

18/39

CONFIDENTIAL.

O. i/c.,
A.G.s Office at the Base,
Central Registry,
ROUEN.

Herewith under Registered Cover War Diary of this Battalion, for the period 1st to 15th March, 1916, the Battalion being amalgamated with the 1/4th Battn. The Black Watch on the latter date.

Kindly acknowledge receipt.

Mur Blair-Irnie
Lieut-Col.,
O.C., 1/5th Bn. The Black Watch, (R.H.).

39th I. B. D.,
A. P. O., Sec. 17.

4th April, 1916.

March
1/5th Bn.   WAR DIARY   The Black Watch
INTELLIGENCE SUMMARY

Place	Date	Hour	Summary of Events and Information	Remarks and references to Appendices
In the Field	1st		The Battn. joined the 118th Inf. Bde under the command of Brig-General W. Bromilaw. The other units in the Brigade being 1/4th BLACK WATCH, 1/6th CHESHIRE REGT, 1/1st CAMBRIDGE REGT, 1/1st HERTS REGT. Capt. T. LYELL rejoined the Battn. to-day.	
	2nd		Capt LYELL assumes command of "A" Company from 1st inst. Coys. paraded under Coy. arrangements.	
	3rd		Battn. under Capt. G.S. RAE paraded for route march. Weather cold and snow fell during the march.	
	4th		The G.O.C., 118th Inf. Bde., was to inspect the Battn. but owing to inclement weather it was postponed. Snow falling heavily during the day.	
	5th		Divine Service was to be held at 10-30 a.m. but owing to the condition of the ground, this had to be abandoned, there being no suitable building for the service.	
	6th		Weather still very unfavourable.	

March

WAR DIARY
INTELLIGENCE SUMMARY.

(Erase heading not required.)

Army Form C. 2118.

Place	Date	Hour	Summary of Events and Information	Remarks and references to Appendices
In the Field	7th Feb		Battn. as part of the 118th Inf. Bde. moved from billets to LA BELLE HOTESSE, STEENBECQUE district, and took over billets there. The weather was bad, snow falling heavily.	
	8th		Billets very scattered and dirty. Snow spoilt any parades to-day, Coys. went for short route marches independantly.	
	9th		As before.	
	10th		Coys. were at the disposal of Os. C. Coys. Weather still inclement.	
	11th		Battn. paraded for Route March under Major CRUICKSHANK, Full Marching Order. A foot inspection being held in the afternoon.	
	12th		There was no Divine Service held owing to the weather conditions.	

March
WAR DIARY
INTELLIGENCE SUMMARY

(Erase heading not required.)

Army Form C. 2118.

Place	Date	Hour	Summary of Events and Information	Remarks and references to Appendices
In the Field	13th		Battn. paraded for Route March under Major RAE.	
	14th		As before, Coys. at disposal of O.C. Coys.	
	15th		The 4th & 5th Battns. THE BLACK WATCH received this order:—	

"Amalgamation".

"The amalgamation of the 1/4th & 1/5th THE BLACK WATCH (R.H.)
"having been completed the Battalion as constituted by the
"Commanding Officers in consultation is approved.
"   The Composite Battalion is placed under the command
"of Lieut-Col. G.A. McL. SCEALES for training and discipline etc.,
"from this date.
"   All surplus personnel will be under the command of
"Lieut-Col. BLAIR-IMRIE, C.M.G., for training and discipline until
"instructions for their disposal is received.
"   The necessary adjustments as regards Pay Lists etc., will
"be carried out forthwith."
(Extract from 118th Inf. Bde. Routine Orders, d/d 15.3.16.)

March

WAR DIARY
or
INTELLIGENCE SUMMARY.
(Erase heading not required.)

Army Form C. 2118.

Place	Date	Hour	Summary of Events and Information	Remarks and references to Appendices
In the Field.	15th		"**Amalgamation**" (contd.) The undermentioned Officers were detailed for duty with the Composite Battalion and formed "C" & "D" Coys. of that unit. "C" Company. Major J. Cruickshank Capt. J. Aubertin. Lieut. J. R. Murray. 2nd Lieut. W. D. MacBeth. 2nd Lieut. J. W. Husband. 2nd Lieut. A. C. Laird. "D" Company. Capt. J. Lyell. Capt. A. H. M. Wedderburn. 2nd Lieut. I. McP. Bain. 2nd Lieut. R. McC. Ritchie. 2nd Lieut. R. C. K. Mill. 2nd Lieut. D. S. Guthrie. Transport Officer - 2nd Lieut. S. S. Paterson. Intelligence Officer - 2nd Lieut. J. C. Forsyth. Adjutant - Capt. & Adjt. J. Kennedy. Warrant Officers :- R.Q.M.S. Milne, Coy. S. M. Baird, Coy. S. M. Burgess, were the Warrant Officers detailed for the Composite Battalion.	

March

WAR DIARY
or
INTELLIGENCE SUMMARY.

(Erase heading not required.)

Army Form C. 2118.

Hour, Date, Place	Summary of Events and Information	Remarks and references to Appendices
In the Field. 15th	"Amalgamation" (cont'd) Lieut. I. M. Bruce-Gardyne was appointed Brigade Grenadier Officer. The undermentioned Officers were detailed as Reinforcements:- Major G. S. Rae. Capt. N. R. Taylor - O.C. "D" Coy. Lieut. R. F. D. Bruce Lieut. (M.) P. S. Duke - O.C. "C" Coy. 2nd Lieut. L. A. Elgood (Adjutant) 2nd Lieut. R. S. L. McPherson. 2nd Lieut. N. A. Grant. 2nd Lieut. K. G. Yarrow. 2nd Lieut. A. Handyside 2nd Lieut. W. McIntyre. Lieut. & Q.M. A. Hall. Regtl. Sgt. Major J. Robertson, Coy. Sgt. Major. G. B. Lowe & Coy. Sgt. Major M. G. Beverly, were the Warrant Officers detailed as Reinforcements.	

March

WAR DIARY
INTELLIGENCE SUMMARY

Hour, Date, Place	Summary of Events and Information	Remarks and references to Appendices

In the Field 15th	"Amalgamation" (cont^d) The number of Other Ranks for duty with the Composite Battalion was as follows:—
	
	                Other Ranks 516
	
	The number of O.R's taken on the strength of 1st Reinforcement was:—
	
	                                    O OR
	            Total taken on strength 15 224
	    O OR
	Less:— Detached for duty with B.M.G. Coy 11
	O/c Forest Control, FORET de NIEPPE. 10
	Salvage Coy. 39th Division. 11
	39th Divnl. Police. 5
	At Base. 1 18
	Employed other places 10 1 65
	                                                14 159
	
	NW Blair-Imrie Lieut-Col.
	O.C. 1/5th Battn. The Black Watch	

www.ingramcontent.com/pod-product-compliance
Lightning Source LLC
Chambersburg PA
CBHW081251170426
43191CB00037B/2115